D0996214

TOOLS OF
TRANSFORMATION

"This book will guide you, inspire you, and provide you with all the tools you'll need to enter the inner world where your truths are found.

Writing is a bridge of transformation, but not always one we know how to cross. This book tells us how."

–Hal Zina Bennett, author of
Write From the Heart

Also by Joanne Klassen

Learning to Live, Learning to Love
Joanne Haynes-Klassen, Jalmar Press, Rolling Hills
Estates, California USA 1985

Pathways to Peace
Bindery Publishing, Winnipeg, MB Canada 1990

Beyond Words
Heartspace Writing School Anthology,
Interior Publishing & Communications Ltd.,
Winnipeg, MB Canada 2002

Seasons of the Heart
Heartspace Writing School Anthology,
Interior Publishing & Communications Ltd.,
Winnipeg, MB Canada 2003

Write Your Way
to New Worlds
of Possibility

–in Just Five Minutes

TOOLS OF
TRANSFORMATION

Joanne Klassen

♥
PAJAMA PRESS CANADA
A HEARTSPACE PUBLICATION

Copyright © 2004 by Joanne Klassen

Design and Layout: Darlene Schacht and Dawn WilsonCover design: Darlene Schacht

ISBN 0-7414-1805-3

Published by:

INFINITY
PUBLISHING.COM

1094 New Dehaven Street
Suite 100
West Conshohocken, PA 19428-2713
Info@buybooksontheweb.com
www.buybooksontheweb.com
Toll-free (877) BUY BOOK
Local Phone (610) 941-9999
Fax (610) 941-9959

Printed in the United States of America

Printed on Recycled Paper

Published June 2004

*This book is dedicated to
the next seven generations.*

*May touching your
truth transform the world.*

INTRODUCTION

What's in it for you to use Tools of Transformation?

WHETHER YOUR JOURNEY of transformation has just begun, you're at a new crossroads, or have been traveling this road for decades, you'll find 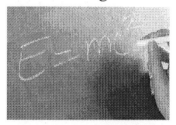 here proven tools to add to your backpack of resources.

Tools of Transformation provides ideas and exercises designed to enrich your relationship with yourself, others, and with the world around you, using writing and awareness as your master tools.

Here you'll find ways to establish an enduring connection to your own creative center.

With these practical approaches you'll be able to:

• Access memory and imagination more quickly.

• Use focusing techniques to guide you beyond distractions and self-criticism.

• Shift your perspective to see new alternatives, and act with more passion and purpose.

Designed for personal and organizational settings, this book blends contemporary research and ancient wisdom to form a map for self-guided tours to new worlds of possibility.

ABOUT HEARTSPACE

HEARTSPACE IS BASED in Winnipeg, Manitoba, Canada near the geographic center of North America. Here two mighty rivers converge. Winnipeg has been a gathering and trading spot for diverse groups for more than a thousand years.

Heartspace creative learning centers are gathering places where diverse groups come to trade the best of what they've discovered about personal and organizational transformation.

I refer to our personal heartspace as the dwelling place of creativity, insight, and rebirth. It is where mind, body, emotions, and Spirit converge.

The basic requirement for the Transformative Process™ is an audience of one—you.

As you write just for you, listen deeply; you'll hear the full-bodied sound of your authentic voice serenading you.

> *Whatever comes from the heart*
> *carries the heat and color*
> *of its birthplace.*
> *~Oliver Wendell Holmes Sr.*

PREFACE

I WRITE MOSTLY for me. I have since I was a kid. Writing's like a partner who gets me dancing and holds me steady through life's whirls and dips.

Because the process of writing has transformed my life, I've wanted to integrate writing into my work as a facilitator of personal and organizational change.

One morning in 1998 I woke up with a clear vision to start Heartspace Writing School. I soon began offering certificate programs in the Transformative Process™. My joy in using this process, the popularity of the programs, and the success stories of Heartspace graduates continue to exceed my dreams.

Four years ago this book tapped me on the shoulder, asking to be born. After pushing it aside again and again, I realized it was time to share this powerful process with a wider audience.

One 92 degree day in Washington, D.C., a bomb scare cut short a problem-solving workshop I was leading. I made a beeline back to the Hotel Topaz, and wrote down ideas for this book, hoping they may help you navigate unexpected curves and crises.

Over dinner that night, I told my oldest daughter, Tiffany, how writing this book was stretching me, the way my belly grew when I was expecting her. Could I find a way to transfer the magic of Heartspace workshops to the printed page? Always my biggest cheerleader, Tiffany urged me on.

There were times when I abandoned this book. When my young nephew ended his life, and cancer threatened my husband Ted, I wrote only to touch my inner lifeline and find full breath again.

When I picked up these pages once more, I was determined to pass along what I discovered about using the Transformative Process™ to tap into reservoirs of strength and insight; to make sense out of good times and hard times.

With each new class, each exhilarating graduation, and each student book launch, I've come to look forward to the moment I'd meet you in these pages.

I hope you'll find *Tools of Transformation* to be like a great dance partner. May these ideas steady you when your world is whirling and dipping. May what you find here bless your steps in this amazing dance we call life. This is what The Transformative Process™ does for me. I wish you abundant success.

Joanne Klassen

And if you get the choice to sit it out
or dance, I hope you dance.
~Mark D. Sanders & Tia Sillers

TABLE OF CONTENTS

PREPARING TO LEARN
THE 3 P'S

Permission
Protection
Potency

PREPARING TO LEARN: THE 3 P'S

Toolbox

**Accelerate Learning with:
Permission, Protection
& Potency**

WHETHER YOU'RE LEARNING to play golf, speak a language, or approach self-discovery through writing, three principles accelerate positive results.

1. **Permission** Give yourself permission to relax. Experiment, ease up—see where this path may lead.

2. **Protection** You can't fail. This is just for you. Choose tools you want to master; set the rest aside.

3. **Potency** You've got blueprints, instructions, exercises, and illustrations to help you succeed.

Freedom is the oxygen of the soul.
~Moshe Dayan

- Commit to learning something you can use from every exercise.
- Keep a pen in your hand and paper close by to capture ideas as you read.
- Apply unfamiliar concepts to familiar situations in your life and career.
- Curb negativity and limit criticism. Look for what's best; leave the rest.
- Have a good time. Learning comes faster and lasts longer when you make it fun.

Playful exploration, openness, and insight will be your best companions for your heartspace journey.

You'll need:

1. A pen and highlighter
2. A notebook and 3 ring binder
3. A timer or clock

What we learn with pleasure we never forget.
~Alfred Mercier

TAKE WHAT'S BEST, LEAVE THE REST

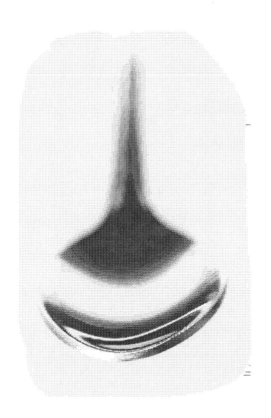

TAKE WHAT'S BEST, LEAVE THE REST

Toolbox

Experiment with all the tools. Hang onto the ones that fit, set the others aside for now.

MOM ALWAYS INSISTED we try a "no-thank-you" bite of unfamiliar vegetables. She'd say, "Just taste it; you might like it after all."

I suggest trying each transformative tool at least once or twice before deciding if it's for you, and then placing it in one of three categories:

1. I like it. I see the potential. I'll use it.
2. I'll see if I can adapt it to work for me.
3. Not for me now. I'll try again later.

> *Taste everything, but swallow only what fits.*
> *- Virginia Satir*

23

Example

Taking Hold of Tools You Can Use

Ed really latched onto the Just 5 Minutes—J5M—tool for timed writing. He found himself whizzing past the inner critic that had slowed his pen to a standstill back in high school. "Writing like this is so easy," he said.

Julie described the discovery of GEMS—Greatest Experienced Moments to Savor, in the String of Story Pearls section, as inner aerobics. "I hum with energy each time I think of one."

Tools of Transformation are as versatile as duct tape. Used alone, each can be a magic wand; or put them together, and who knows what will happen. Play with the tools like a kid investigating the treasure in Grandma's attic.

Tom Sawyer said, "Work is what a body's obliged to do, and play is what a body is not obliged to do."

Think of each activity as an **invitation**, never as an **expectation**. See what matches your mood. Go at your own pace. Take what's best and leave the rest.

> *You can't leave footprints in the sands of time*
> *if you're sitting on your butt.*
> *And who wants to leave butt prints*
> *in the sands of time?*
> *~Bob Moawad*

TOOL 1

J5M
Just Five Minutes

Just Five Minutes: J5M

Toolbox

**Transformative
change begins within
—just five minutes at a time.**

HAVE YOU EVER wondered how some people achieve
the near-impossible? I learned about J5M from
just such a person. My friend Meira Lofchick and
I solved the problems of our lives as we walked
through the neighborhood, talking and stopping
for tea.

One day at a visit to Meira's neurologist, she
was told that because of the progression of
multiple sclerosis, weight-bearing exercise should
be discontinued. What were we going to do? I
enjoy almost any exercise except swimming. Sure
enough, swimming popped into her mind and
Meira arranged for us to use the swimming pool at
her sister's apartment building.

The first afternoon, we each swam laps in adjoining lanes of the pool. After 10 minutes, Meira swam to the side of the pool and said, "That's all I can do." Fine with me; we had a shower and stopped for tea and talk. Not too bad.

The next time at the pool, after 10 minutes I started toward the side. Meira said, "I'm going to see if I can go just five more minutes today."

I joined her. Within a month, we were swimming over a mile, then two.

From Meira I learned the power of just 5 minutes to transform a life. Some days we couldn't even go the original 10 minutes, but we established a pattern that carried us forward.

When my days are full to overflowing and there doesn't seem to be time for me, I've learned that I can squeeze J5M between other activities, and, in those magic moments, reconnect with the best in myself.

I wrote this book in J5M increments. After wedging in the first five minutes, I found that I could often continue writing for longer blocks of time, but always five minutes at a time.

A mountain-climber friend tells me that, like writing, the secret to scaling a daunting slope is not taking huge strides, but one small step followed by another.

Each Tool has a section of "hands-on" exercises for you to complete in the book or in your notebook or binder.

When you see this symbol: in the margin, it signals an exercise to give you a chance to practice using the tool. You'll find examples interspersed among exercises.

Each exercise begins with the number of the tool and a letter; A, B, C, etc. These references will come in handy if you want to organize your exercises in a binder.

J5M Exercises

1A

When I think I can't do something, I've found that telling myself, "Just 5 minutes, Joanne," can kick start new waves of energy that sometimes last for hours.

What would you like to do that you don't think you can?

What is one thing you could do, a small step in the direction of your desire?

Do it for J5M right now, and when you return, write about the results.

1B

Taking J5M for something I really don't want to do can trick me into getting it done.

It helped me gather all my financial records to take to the accountant at income tax time, a chore I dread.

What jobs do you really not want to do? List a few.

Begin one aspect of a dreaded chore for J5M as an experiment and see what happens.

Return to write about what you became aware of in the process.

1c

I'd always intended to walk down the stairs to pick up my mail instead of taking the elevator. I started with, "I'll just take the stairs for J5M." I ended up walking down all 10 flights.

What's one thing you've intended to do but haven't found time for?

Today, spend J5M to break new ground and note what you discovered.

1D

On a winter morning when the alarm goes off, one of my favorite treats is to snuggle under the warmth of the covers for five more minutes before getting up.

Identify a secret life-enriching pleasure to extend by J5M.

 What's it like to do it?

1E

Recently, I stopped by the duck pond at a nearby park and watched the ducklings for just five minutes on a very disappointing day. Later, I found I could teach my evening class with an upbeat attitude, something that would have been a struggle otherwise.

What natural setting is available to you where you can reconnect with nature or wildlife?

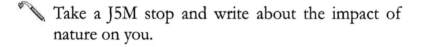 Take a J5M stop and write about the impact of nature on you.

1F

Writers who find themselves in a staring contest with a blank page find that they can duck the censorship of the inner critic with thoughts of, "I'll just write for 5 minutes."

Soon they've slid under the radar of fear's gatekeeper to discover that they've snuck in an hour or more of writing.

Pick up your pen and paper or a journal and write like the wind, starting with "If I write for just five minutes..."

1G

I once read that the average time a child is listened to is less than 3 minutes a day. When my daughter, Tiffany, was small, if I was distracted when she was talking to me, she'd sometimes take my face between her hands so that I'd look at her. This helped me put other activities on pause for J5M to hear what was important to her.

Who is waiting or hoping to be heard by you?

Who do you want to be heard by?

Commit to listening for J5M without interrupting. Have a conversation with someone now, by phone or in person.

 What was it like? Write about what you noticed.

1H

My friend Georgia once came to visit me in
Winnipeg from her home in Ann Arbor, Michigan.
I couldn't help but notice how lovely she looked in
the morning. What was her beauty secret?

Georgia told me she spends five minutes counting
her blessings before she gets out of bed.

Experiment with this J5M tool to jump-start joy
anytime of day or night. See how you look in the
mirror while thinking blessing thoughts.

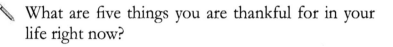 What are five things you are thankful for in your
life right now?

1ɪ

When my younger daughter, Anna, was the manager of a busy health food store, she often didn't have time for a break. She'd stand at the store counter with a pen and paper and calm down by making lists; things to take along on a camping trip or other things she was looking forward to. She said it kept her from getting listless.

For a pick-me-up, write a list of things you enjoy doing, for J5M.

1J

Have you ever memorized a poem, verse, song, or scripture? Many people know the 23rd Psalm, or David's Psalm, a poem from school days, or John Lennon's song, Imagine, for example.

As a mini-meditation, invest J5M in repetition of a positive, lyrical verse and notice how your breathing slows and your muscles begin to relax.

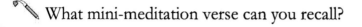 What mini-meditation verse can you recall?

TOOL 2

Write Now...Freestyle

WRITE NOW...FREESTYLE

Toolbox

Write fast and free.
Forget the rules for now.

BECAUSE I LOVE to write, and I founded a writing school, I encounter many writers. I believe that everyone is born to write, to express a unique view of the world. People have been naming their experiences, sharing stories on the walls of caves and around the fire since the first man and woman disagreed about who did what.

> *Have compassion for yourself when you write.*
> *There is no failure - just a big field to wander in.*
> *~Natalie Goldberg*

School helped many kids learn the joy of writing from teachers who loved the written word. Unfortunately, some teachers approached writing less as a means of creative self-expression, and more as an opportunity to encourage perfection. Thus, the famous "red pen" was enlisted to put errant letters, thoughts, and punctuation back in line.

It is a damned poor mind indeed that can't think
of at least two ways of spelling any word.
~Andrew Jackson

At Heartspace Writing School, red pens are banned. The process of writing takes precedence over the product of writing.

Write to find joy in capturing live thoughts, feelings, and experiences—your voice—on the page.

Freestyle writing was invented long ago to help novice, pro, and reluctant writers fill blank pages with ease.

Think of Freestyle writing as free association.

Forget about pleasing an audience, topic sentences, complete sentences, punctuation, spelling, and making sense. This is a place for you to catch up with yourself.

If, later, you are dazzled by the wit or wisdom of what you've written, editing can ensure that your writing is squeaky clean before it leaves you to go out into the world.

Your life is like a book filled with blank pages.
You can fill them with anything you choose.
What will it be?
~Joanne Klassen

Tips before you write on...

Using a quiet timer when you write will let you forget about watching the clock so you can devote full attention to writing.

You may find that using the blank spaces in the book, or a spiral notebook, works well for shorter exercises.

When you write longer pieces, a 3-ring binder will come in handy. It makes it easy to organize your writing into sections and move pages around freely.

Privacy and Intellectual Property —Something to think about.

I heard about a woman who lost a box when she moved that contained years of her writing, her poems, and journal entries. She didn't have her name on them.

She'd written just for herself and didn't even think about signing her name. Someone found, and successfully published, her poems and reflections. She had to go to great lengths to prove that she was the author.

For safe keeping, save your private writing in a secure place. Put your name somewhere on each piece, along with the date, time, and place.

J5M Freestyle Exercises

You aim your hand toward the page and
affirm the life flowing through your veins.
~Carryn Mirriam-Goldberg

For each of these exercises, set your timer, or notice how much you usually write in five minutes, and use that as your guideline.

Write your response to each exercise as quickly as you can, without stopping, for five minutes. When you finish, re-read, using your highlighter to mark the essence of what you've written. Feel free to make lists, draw pictures, write in point form, or write sideways on the page, as you wish.

Extending your hand is extending yourself.
~Rod McKuen

2A

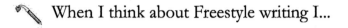 When I think about Freestyle writing I...

2B

 Write a letter to yourself from an angel or spiritual being who wants to tell you why it is important to your transformation for you to write.

2c

Compose a Freestyle verse or poem comparing your personal qualities to a garden or something growing.

Example

She didn't need much tending, unlike the fussy flowers—just soil, moisture, and some sunlight. Not necessarily direct or indirect sunlight, just sunlight. She weathered the longest, coldest winters Manitoba is famous for, and could be counted on to emerge every spring, in profusion, sometimes popping up, gracing unexpected, unadorned places. Was it easy to take her for granted? I suppose so.

2D

 Describe a favorite childhood toy and the fun that you associate with getting it and playing with it.

2e

 Write about your pet peeves, fears, or worries.

2F

 Write about the most perfect or nearly perfect day you can remember or imagine.

2G

Describe the inner and outer qualities that you cherish about someone near and dear to you.

2H

 Write as many things as you can think of that begin
with, "Most people don't realize that I..."

2J

What is your fantasy vacation or trip? Describe it in as much detail as possible.

2K

Close your eyes and revisit a kitchen you spent time
in as a child.

Look around for sights, smells, sounds, and
objects.

Pick one and start writing about it as if you were
sitting or standing in that kitchen now.

TOOL 3

Awareness is Power

AWARENESS IS POWER:

Toolbox

**The Prime Power tool
is Awareness.
Awareness is Power
The power to choose
The power to change &
The power to create.**

TRANSFORMATION REQUIRES CONSCIOUSLY choosing a life-enriching focus just 5 minutes more today than yesterday.

- Awareness provides the power of choice. Transformation means identifying and changing patterns that limit aliveness.

- Awareness plugs in the power to change. Transformation involves finding the gain from past pain and moving forward with forgiveness.

- Awareness is the power source for creating new patterns of possibility.

**New perspectives give birth to new beliefs—
the lifeblood of transformation.**

> *To be in hell is to drift.*
> *To be in heaven is to steer.*
> *~George Bernard Shaw*

Many of the tools and exercises in *Tools of Transformation* begin by reaching for the prime power tool: awareness. Here are 10 ways to increase self-awareness right now, in five minutes. Start with just five minutes; you may choose to go on from there.

In this book or in your notebook, write as if you are clearing your mind by sweeping your thoughts onto the page. I call this "Clearing Writing." It's a simple way to strengthen your awareness muscles.

When you finish, scan your notes and highlight anything you want to remember, or the essence of your thoughts at this moment.

I suggest entering the date, time, and place as you write. I found an entry I wrote at 9:00 a.m. on September 11, 2001. The world changed forever that day. Without the a.m. notation, my perspective would make a lot less sense when I read it later.

Awareness Exercises

3A

Mentally create an "Awareness Scale" with #1 as the worst day of your life, and #10 as the best.

Give yourself a score as of this moment.

#1_____#10

Note the things that are influencing your score both upward and downward.

What can you leave behind that will help you move even higher?

3B

Notice your posture, how you are standing, sitting, or lying.

Scan from the tips of your toes, paying particular attention to tension, all the way up to the top of your head. Pause to take a deep breath.

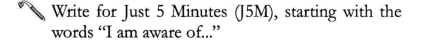 Write for Just 5 Minutes (J5M), starting with the words "I am aware of..."

3c

Three Key Questions

We each have our own reasons for starting something new.

The clearer we are about these reasons, and the match between the reasons, timing, and the approach we choose, the more likely we are to find satisfaction and success.

On a sheet of paper, write today's date and time, then for just five minutes, write whatever thoughts come to mind in response to these three key questions:

Why me?
Why this?
Why now?

Debrief

What became clear to you as you wrote your answers? Did you find that thoughts flowed freely from your mind to the page, or was something holding you back?

Return to these questions again and again to polish your perspective on why transformation is important to you.

3D

If you were to describe yourself right this minute, as some form of water, what would best describe you?

Start writing and continue for J5M (just 5 minutes). Include sensory details about the form you'd take, what it's like, and how your choice relates to your life right now.

Example

A J5M Comparison

I'm like a thin crust of ice on a puddle, waiting for a child's red rubber boot to pounce and open me up.

I'm not chilly by nature, but coolness has settled in since betrayal shattered my daughter's world. I have been frosting over a bit, keeping a distance from people, even those closest to me. I am waiting for spring, for new life and breakthroughs. For child-like energy to return and shatter isolation, melt me back into the flow of life.

Debrief

What was it like for you to compare yourself to something else?

Creative insight often comes from comparing things that are not usually combined.

3E

Listen for the furthest sound you can hear.

Filter out sounds, one at a time, from far to near.

For J5M, write, in sequence, about each sound you can identify and its impact on you.

Example

Awareness of Sound

Five Minute Symphony

The crickets, first sound to embrace my ears, remind me of a squeaky piece of machinery that needs a drop of WD40. They soon provide a certain comforting background canopy as I lie here in Tiffany's hammock on a sunny October afternoon in Keedysville, Maryland.

Now layers of sound compete, each with its own tempo. A bee buzzes at close range, zeroing in on my plump, juicy red grapes. A dog barks two doors down and is answered by a canine chum, or bum, a block away. Birds cawing overhead remind me of a domestic dispute. The hum of a lawnmower across the way signals the presence of an industrious neighbor.

A jet drones overhead, slicing the sky. Cars whiz by. Tiffy clinks dishes, emptying the dishwasher, near where I lie. My stomach gurgles, remembering the rich fruit flan Luke brought for her birthday celebration.

As I listen more closely, I hear another bird's wee, sweet, high-pitched song. Someone hammers on and on. A rural mailbox is opened, closed. A door slams, a motorcycle revs. A warm breeze ruffles leaves on the towering beech tree over yonder. Now, in the near silence, I catch the rhythmic sound of my own breath.

In the stillness, the crickets commence. A soft, muffled woman's voice quiets a baby's cry. A distant train whistle upstages all else, commanding attention.

"Surround sound," world-class acoustics, unrivaled by the latest technology, reign here in my daughter's Eden-like garden in tiny rural Keedysville. Church bells, playing their hourly, familiar heartwarming hymn, remind me just how close to heaven my ears and I have been. My five-minute journey into listening, just plain old doing-nothing listening, has given this weary traveler an impromptu symphony to remember.

© Joanne Klassen, 1:45 p.m. Mon. 10/22/01
Keedysville, MD, USA

3F

Look around—360 degrees.

Now, close your eyes and think of a color.

Open your eyes and notice everything in any shade of your color.

Write for J5M, starting with the words, "I became aware of..." and expand on your experience.

3G

Become aware of the feel of every texture touching your skin.

Notice the textures that surround you and mentally touch several of them.

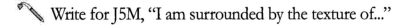 Write for J5M, "I am surrounded by the texture of..."

Include the impact of the textures you became aware of, such as the sharp edge of the shirt label skimming the back of your neck.

3H

Notice all sources of light that surround you.

Be aware of where the light comes from, how it falls, what is illuminated and what is in shadow.

Write for J5M about your awareness of light and about the impact of light on you right here, right now.

What are the sources of lightness or brightness in your life these days?

What are the sources of darkness or shadow?

31

If you could have any beverage or snack right now, what would suit your mood?

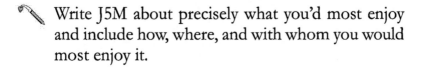 Write J5M about precisely what you'd most enjoy and include how, where, and with whom you would most enjoy it.

3J

Compare your present mood to weather, such as a gentle, refreshing rain shower, a downpour, or monsoon, the northern lights on a clear night, etc.

Write as if you are that weather, starting with the words "I am..."

TOOL 4

Inner Influences

Inner Influences

Toolbox
Learn to identify the inner voices that encourage or inhibit your personal transformation.

WITHIN EACH PERSON resides a chorus of voices that can be encouraging and affirming; critical or censoring; rational or objective; curious and exploratory; or fearful and cautious. Dr. Eric Berne identified various aspects of personality in the 1960's. He called his work Transactional Analysis.

You can side-step unnecessary barriers by being able to identify or analyze the various voices of inner influences. What are the messages each part has for you about personal change?

- **Encourager:** cheerleader; nurturing, caring, comforting, warm, understanding, reassuring, supportive, and affirming.

- **Critical Censor:** controlling, disciplining, prejudicial, prohibitive, protective, punitive, authoritative, and rigid.
  Concerned with safety, judgment, rules.

77

- **Objective Advisor:** receives, analyzes, and integrates data. Logical, reasonable, relaxed, systematic, and rational.

- **Curious Creator:** experimental, "Wonder Child"; child-like, imaginative, intuitive, playful, spontaneous, sensuous, energetic, uninhibited, expressive, and creative.

- **Cautious Follower:** conforming; wants to please; resigned, rebellious at times, and fearful.

At a writing workshop with Hal Zina Bennet, author of *Write from the Heart*, we were asked to write from the perspective of an inner encourager, a voice of someone who was likely to give us positive messages about ourselves.

Here is what I wrote in a 20-minute writing exercise. The words attributed to my Aunt Phid were never actually spoken; I invented them.

Example

My Encourager

My Aunt Phid is one of those people who waltzes into your childhood just when you need her most and makes up for what's missing.

With six children of her own, Lord knows how she found time to make me feel special as I sat on the stool by the sink with her patiently dipping the comb in a jelly glass of water as she French braided my hair.

Talking to me about everyday moments in her life and making thick chocolate milkshakes for just the two of us helped to build the foundation upon which my sense of self worth stands today.

Her death several years ago from cancer cannot take away the aliveness of the love that lives afresh with each thought of my encourager.

Join us in her cozy, crowded kitchen on Maple Street in Des Moines, Iowa, as she tells her four sisters about my writing.

"Wait till you read Joey's writing! I was laughing and wiping tears on my sleeve the whole time. It won't take long and you'll feel like she really knows you.

Joey just seems to sense things that are happening inside people. Things you may never have seen or even thought of.

Joey seems like she is in another world a lot of the time, and when you read what she writes you'll be glad she is and that she writes about it. It's familiar, yet different.

Seems like she's listening and figuring out things most of us miss or we're just so used to that we never bother to think about. She climbs inside situations, like going down in the well and letting you know what it's like down there. It's really interesting—like magic.

Suddenly Pop is a lion—king of the jungle. Roaring. Maybe he does feel out of control with his blood sugar going all over the place. We think he's just being mean to Ma and we try to get him to stop yelling. Joey sees him like a scared little kid with the Indianapolis 500 running through his body. He wants Ma to make it stop so he hollers at her about her cooking or any old thing. You see? She sees it differently than we do. Kind of makes you think.

She sees each of us kids calling out for love in our own way and that just makes me want to cry. She feels real sad when we talk about her mom, Peggy. She wants us to see her the way she does, as good and strong and courageous, not snooty because she has an education.

When I read Joey's writing I feel like I am a good person. She believes so much in people's basic goodness that you want to believe it and see it that way too.

We don't talk about God or anything like that much in this family, but somehow she makes it seem like something good is behind the scenes and at the heart of it all. Not corny, or rubbing your nose in it, just clear common sense anybody can understand.

Reading her words reminds me of lighting the lantern or sitting around the fire—you just feel good and not so alone. She doesn't mind telling about the rough stuff, but in a gentle way, not ugly. Did you know that she wanted to die when she came to live with Ma? Just this little kid and all those big feelings.

Maybe our kids are like that. Feeling lots of stuff they can't tell anybody about and having to make sense of it for themselves.

I wish I could write like that. Honestly, it's amazing. Who knows where it comes from? Joey says she just listens and it sort of taps her on the shoulder and says 'write this down.' I'm really glad she does. See if she'll let you read a little. You'll love it."

After I wrote this I felt like I'd turned a corner and began to see my writing in a more positive new light.

Inner Influences Exercises

4A

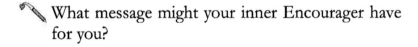 What message might your inner Encourager have for you?

Don't skimp on praise, and include as many specifics as you can.

4B

What does your Critical Censor have to say?

4c

 What do you think your Objective Advisor would want you to remember about personal change ?

4D

What can you do to include your inner Wonder Child or Curious Creator in your process of change?

Make a list of a dozen things your Wonder Child loves to do. Keep adding to it.

Decorate your binder with pictures that delight you.

4E

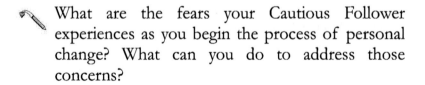 What are the fears your Cautious Follower experiences as you begin the process of personal change? What can you do to address those concerns?

Have you noticed that your Cautious Follower rebels at times? What form does this take?

Tool 5

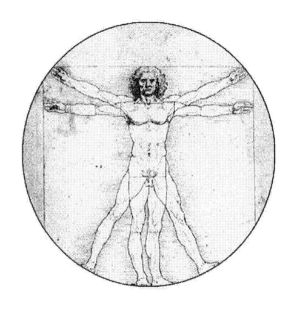

Anatomy of an Experience

_____ **Toolbox** _____

ANATOMY OF AN EXPERIENCE

EVENT

FILTER
Values + Past Experiences =
an Assessment, Interpretation,
Perception or Point of View,
which activates a belief

BELIEFS

THOUGHTS

FEELINGS

PHYSICAL SENSATIONS

ACTIONS / BEHAVIORS

REACTION

OUTCOME / EXPERIENCES

IT MAY NOT be possible to control the events of our lives, but many things go into creating an experience, and they are within our control.

When one aspect of an experience changes, the whole experience changes.

The Anatomy of an Experience describes the various stages we travel through as we turn events into experiences.

When an event occurs, our mind instantly filters new information through our values and past experiences to arrive at a perception, which activates a belief, or what we see as true.

The sum of what we call an experience is:

- An event occurs
- It's viewed through a filter based on values, past experiences, and expectations
- Which gives us our perception
- Which activates a belief
- Which generates thoughts
- Which lead to feelings
- Which become physical sensations
- Which motivate actions or behaviors

This all happens inside us, and is our response to events. Our behaviors engender the reactions of others, which result in outcomes.

Example

I've always struggled with math. When I got a B on my report card back in high school, I thought it was a miracle; my prayers were answered. I was elated and called my friend, Linda, a straight A student. She got a B in math on her report card and expressed anger and disappointment. She thought the teacher had made a mistake. She couldn't understand my excitement and was irritated with me. Though Linda and I experienced the same event, we had very different experiences based on our expectations and perception. Linda still remembers how bad she felt with that B on her record.

After a traffic accident, police officers interview eyewitnesses to get a composite picture of what actually happened. People who just witnessed the same event report several versions of the accident.

Imagine how difficult it is to discern the truth, especially of past events. Yet, like Linda, we often cling to limiting beliefs and judgments of ourselves and others based on incomplete data, or interpretations, sometimes for years.

Life is a mirror,
and what you see out there,
you must first see inside yourself.
~Wally "Famous" Amos

Another example is Mandy. When I saw her carrying her toddler into church, I noticed that the baby's soft blonde locks had been replaced by a short, spiky haircut. When I asked about it she told me that her husband thought that brushing their daughter's hair would be easier on the baby and on them if he cut it, which he did while Mandy was grocery shopping.

Remembering how I looked forward to my baby's first haircut, I thought I'd probably be upset, so I asked Mandy how she felt.

"At first I was annoyed," she said. "Then I asked myself, 'Why would I want to be angry about something like this?' There's nothing I can do about the haircut. It's only hair and it will grow back."

I've never forgotten her words or the question, **"Why would I want to be angry about this?"**

The only real voyage of discovery
consists not in seeking new landscapes
but in having new eyes.
~Marcel Proust

When we're not comfortable with someone else's behavior, we have four choices:

1. Get the other person to change.
2. Change the situation or circumstances in which the behavior occurs.
3. Leave, temporarily or permanently, mentally or physically.
4. Change our interpretation of the behavior and our response to it.

The first can be like trying to move a massive boulder, compared to the last, which can be more like removing a pesky pebble from your shoe.

When we combine the Anatomy map with Awareness, our prime power tool, we can see how we've chosen a particular perspective. Like Mandy with her daughter's haircut, we can choose another way to look at a situation.

The Anatomy of an Experience illustrates the entry points of change, from perception to outcomes. It is easier to change your belief, which is at the start of the Anatomy map, than the reactions of others, which are at the bottom.

Beliefs are like radio towers: they transmit thousands of thought signals almost simultaneously. The signals begin the flow of thoughts along a particular channel or line of thinking that follows perception.

I thrive on order, which is a challenge because both Ted and I are pack rats. I like to keep the island counter in our kitchen clutter-free. Ted and the kids set keys, cell phones, mail, backpacks —whatever— on the counter. I used to fuss about how important it was to me to keep the counter clear.

Recently I realized that the island counter is a natural magnet for messes. I've changed my perspective and have begun to see my job as de-clutterer of that counter. I place the stuff that ends up there on a bench by the door and say, "I like to keep the counter cleaned off. Your things are on the bench." This honors their needs and mine. It's a small transformation, but a step toward creating peace.

Sometimes we shift perception in a negative direction without intending to.

Awareness gives us the power to recognize the signals of distress and shift to another view point.

Example

Event, Filter, Belief

> *I learned in April 2002 that my husband Ted had prostate cancer. I suggested that we adopt the motto, "We are not afraid." My belief is that each of us might be afraid separately, but together we would be strong. We believe in natural and holistic approaches, so Ted began several alternative therapies to address his condition.*

> *Words are, of course, the most*
> *powerful drug used by mankind.*
> ~Rudyard Kipling

Example

Shift in Perception =
New Belief, Thoughts & Feelings

> *In May, when an oncologist told us that Ted had stage 4 cancer and should begin radiation treatment immediately, my point of view shifted, activated by a belief that immediate medical intervention was necessary. So much for "we are not afraid." I was scared that Ted would die.*

Thoughts become "self talk"—what we tell ourselves to be true. We think something like 50,000 thoughts a day, and most of them are a recycling of the same thoughts we've had before.

Thoughts generate feelings. Thus, thinking, "The doctor knows best," activated my fear of losing Ted unless he started radiation immediately.

Emotions become embodied as sensations. Physical sensations like anxiety or tension seek release and cause action.

Example

Physical Sensations,
Actions, and Reaction

I couldn't sleep, began craving sweets, and called cancer centers across North America. As I kept busy gathering information, Ted and I grew further apart.

One day I read an article that talked about the small number of cancer cells in comparison to the healthy cells in the body. It suggested concentrating on strengthening and celebrating the healthy cells. Bingo! My perspective shifted, a new belief was available, and my self-talk began to travel along different pathways. I relaxed and stopped obsessing about cancer and treatment.

> *Do not be conformed to this world,*
> *but be transformed by*
> *the renewing of your mind...*
> *~Romans 12: 1,2 The Bible*

My new belief instantly empowered me with positive thoughts, joyful enthusiasm, and renewed vigor in the same circumstances in which I'd been laden with fear.

Ted went on to have more diagnostic tests and eventually had radiation targeted to a more specific area than was first suggested.

> *We see things not as they are,*
> *we see them as we are.*
> *~The Talmud*

As the Anatomy of an Experience shows, what we do influences how other people react to us.

Example

New Perception
= New Outcomes

When I shifted my perception to focus on Ted's health and vitality instead of his illness, a new closeness sprang up between us. We resumed our Saturday breakfast dates, a treat we'd let slide.

As we approach personal and organizational transformation five minutes at a time, the Anatomy of an Experience is a useful map to our interior territory. Much like a mechanic's view beneath the hood of a car, it clarifies how all the elements work together to produce a result.

For many years, I was a stress management consultant. I came to see shifting perception as the goldmine of stress mastery.

As we understand our role in creating experiences, we can use the next tool, the Transformative Process™, as a step-by-step guide to change.

We have the power to choose to transform painful experiences using a new lens of perception.

As we intentionally look for ways to see things differently, we are guaranteed to find positive alternatives.

Leaving behind the baggage of fear-based, limiting beliefs frees up energy to create more life-enriching future experiences.

If the door of perception were cleansed,
everything would appear to man as it is, infinite.
~William Blake

Summary

Our lives are made up of countless experiences. Perception is fluid, like water. The tap is within our control.

Intention is the compass that guides our awareness toward a chosen destination.

Awareness is like a flashlight that we shine on perception.

Tools of Transformation provides a step-by-step pathway to help us master change.

Anatomy of an Experience Exercises

5A

Consider Mandy's response to her husband cutting their baby's hair, "Why would I want to be angry about that?"

Identify a situation in which you've found yourself feeling angry or annoyed.

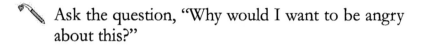 Ask the question, "Why would I want to be angry about this?"

Write the thoughts that come in response.

5B

Select a relationship in which you don't feel as comfortable as you'd like.

Remember the police officer at the scene of an accident. Place yourself in the shoes of several people who witness the relationship between you and the person you're uncomfortable with.

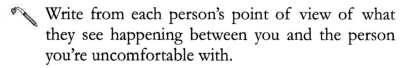 Write from each person's point of view of what they see happening between you and the person you're uncomfortable with.

5c

Like Ted and I, when he was diagnosed with cancer, you have had experiences that have generated fear in your life.

What kind of self-talk feeds your fearful perceptions?

What were some of the physical sensations and symptoms that you noticed when fear was active?

5D

Remember a time when you read or heard something that gave you a new view on a troubling issue in your life—like the article that I read comparing the number of unhealthy cells in the body to its large number of strong, vital cells.

What was the result of the new view for you?

How did it change your experience of the troubling event or circumstance?

5E

Are there positive habits, like my Saturday breakfast dates with Ted, that you've let slip?

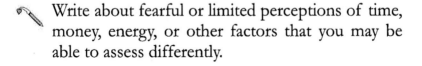 Write about fearful or limited perceptions of time, money, energy, or other factors that you may be able to assess differently.

5F

 What kinds of changes have you seen in organizations you are associated with when new perspectives, either possibility-driven or fear-driven, have been introduced?

5G

When I tried to get my family and friends to stop putting things on the island in the kitchen, I found myself fighting an uphill battle, while telling myself that they didn't care about my comfort. It wasn't true.

Identify a situation where you are still trying to get someone else to change his or her behavior in relation to you.

Explore several ways you might change your response, including changing your expectations or actions.

5H

Imagine someone you respect telling you about a painful event in their early life that is similar to something you experienced, except that they are telling you about how it turned out to contain many hidden blessings.

Write about your experience, telling about hidden blessings that came from your painful experience.

51

Outdated values can lurk just out of reach of our conscious mind.

I have a hard time leaving the house without making the bed, even when no one else will see my bed before I return. When I sacrifice time from something that matters more than making the bed, I become aware that I'm governed by an outdated value about having my bed made before leaving the house.

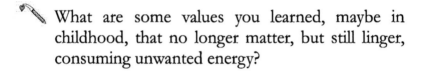 What are some values you learned, maybe in childhood, that no longer matter, but still linger, consuming unwanted energy?

5J

Expectations are at the heart of perception.

Defensive behavior is the result of expecting to be criticized and projecting judgment and criticism when there may be none.

Are there any kinds of judgment you expect, or find yourself reacting to, that rarely occur?

Write about the type of criticism that you're most uncomfortable with.

TOOL 6

The Transformative Process™

The Transformative Process™

 Toolbox

For personal or organizational transformation:

Name experiences without shame
Claim them without blame
Tame them without complaining
Reframe them without explaining
Proclaim them without restraining

THE STEPS IN the Transformative Process™ allow us to move forward with awareness, using the compass of positive intention, to create new possibilities, just five minutes at a time.

Naming

The first of the five stages or steps is **Naming** an experience without shame. This step is the starting point for accurately and respectfully examining our experiences.

The goal of this stage is to describe an event, including our perspective, beliefs, thoughts, feelings, sensations, actions and reactions as precisely and completely as possible in J5M.

Feelings are neither right nor wrong; they are facts in themselves.

When Anna says, "I'm so stressed," she's naming her present reality. If I'm aware, and my intention is to respect her, I can accept that this is how she feels at the moment. I don't need to try to cheer her up or get her to see things differently.

As a child, when I said I was angry, my mother would say, "You're just tired." This was her perception. Today, I seldom think of myself as angry, just tired. It's been hard for me to identify and name anger.

Example

Naming an Experience,
without Shame

When I was asked to help a re-build a team after a beloved leader left, I asked team members to name their present experience, without shame, in J5M.

One woman wrote: "She (the leader) was the glue that held us together. We fight like children. I believe we could eat each other up, and I dread coming to work. I am afraid I'll lose my job because I'm numb and I don't care any more. I have withdrawn from the others, who seem suspicious of me. It's like we've all become enemies."

Regardless of whether we've had the exact experience of another person, only a limited number of emotions exist and we've all felt those emotions to one degree or another since childhood.

Emotions are the common ground that allows us to connect with experiences quite different from our own.

The Five Basic Feelings are:

Mad
Sad,
Glad,
Hurt &
Scared

All other emotions are a combination of these feelings—all, that is, except guilt. Guilt isn't an emotion at all—it's a word used to describe what we think someone else expects us to feel.

Learning to name experiences fully can be liberating even if you don't continue on to use the other steps in the Transformative Process™.

Naming an experience is where change starts. Set your timer for J5M and begin with the first question.

Naming Exercises

6A

Name an upsetting experience as specifically, accurately, and honestly as you can, without shame.

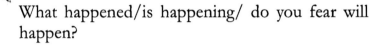

What happened/is happening/ do you fear will happen?

6B

Filter

What's in your Filter: Past Experiences, values, expectations, assessment, interpretation, and point of view.

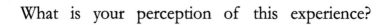

What is your perception of this experience?

6c

Beliefs

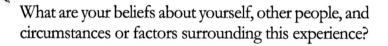

What are your beliefs about yourself, other people, and circumstances or factors surrounding this experience?

6D

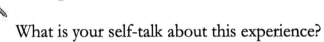

Thoughts

What is your self-talk about this experience?

6E

Feelings

Examine your feelings: mad, sad, glad, hurt, scared, or a combination of these.

What are your feelings related to this?

6F

Physical Sensations

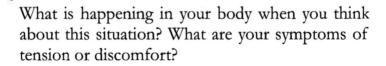

What is happening in your body when you think about this situation? What are your symptoms of tension or discomfort?

6G

Actions

What are your behaviors associated with this situation?

6H

Reactions

What are other people's reactions toward you as a result of this experience?

61

Summary

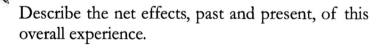

Describe the net effects, past and present, of this overall experience.

6J

Past Experience

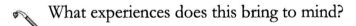 What experiences does this bring to mind?

What could you compare it to?

Claiming

The next step is **Claiming** an experience without blame.

No one is blamed, including ourselves.

Blame fuels victimization, anger, and resentment—a downward spiral that results in a sense of powerlessness.

If any of these feelings are present, power is being given away. Change can take place only when we claim responsibility for our own experiences.

Forgiveness is freedom.

Example

Claiming an Experience,
Without Blame

In the claiming stage, the team member I mentioned wrote:

"My experience is not about others on the team. They are having their own challenges, based on who they are. This is my personal struggle. My perception creates my experience. I want to change how I view this so that I have more choices."

Claiming Exercises

6к

Is there anyone you are blaming for this experience or pattern?

If so, Who? How? Why?

6L

If you stopped blaming, and claimed that you are the person whose perception is creating this reaction, what might happen?

6M

What are your present perceptions and judgments costing you?

 What do you get out of hanging on to this?

6N

 Finish this sentence, "I know that is about me, not about someone else because...."

60

When you read the words, "We see things not as they are but as we are," what are your thoughts?

Taming

The third Transformative step is **Taming** our experiences without complaining.

Complaining is another way of expending negative energy; pushing people away; fueling anger, resentment, and powerlessness.

Taming requires us to uncover the roots of the belief underlying the experience. Taming starts with detective work. We are searching for limiting or painful conditioning and values that created the outdated beliefs that may be lurking beneath our awareness, like a tiger waiting to pounce.

This is done without complaining about how the belief came to be. A signal that taming is underway is when we stop defending painful perspectives —the magnets for faulty, incomplete evidence.

A question I have found helpful for taming is: **What would someone have to believe in order to have this kind of experience?**

Example

Taming Without Complaining

This time the woman in the team building session searched to find the belief that was the powder keg that caused the explosion of fear she'd been experiencing. After a few minutes she wrote, "When someone in charge leaves, bad things will happen."

Then she wrote, "Where is this belief coming from?" What came to mind was the chaos bordering on abuse that she experienced when her older siblings were left in charge when their mother returned to work. It felt to her like they might eat each other up.

Another helpful questions is: "Why would I want to continue living with the consequences of this belief?"

In taming an experience, it can help to compare what is now with past experiences.

What is there about this situation that's the same as a painful past experience, and how is this different?

Taming Exercises

6P

 What would someone have to believe in order to have this kind of experience?

6Q

Where does this belief come from?

6R

Why would you want to continue living with these consequences?

6s

Compare this experience to a common, emotionally charged situation; for example,

"I felt like a kid on my first day of Kindergarten. I wanted to be there, and I wanted to go home."

Reframing

The fourth Transformative step is **Reframing** the experience without explaining.

This step is like taking an old photograph out of one frame and putting it into a new one. It looks different.

Example

Reframing Without Explaining

Ted sometimes accuses me of telling him what I don't want (blaming/complaining) rather than specifying what I do want.

When I say, "How many times have I told you, please don't put your stuff on the kitchen counter. I feel like this place is out of control when it's all messed up." He'd prefer that I said, "Will you please put your things on the bench. I like to keep the counter clear."

Going into unnecessary detail—explaining the what, why and how of a perspective—is a means of self-protection. It drains our energy, and the energy of others.

The key question in Reframing is:

What do I want instead of this?

- In my new reality, what would I believe?
- What would I think?
- What would I feel?
- What would my body sensations be?
- What would I be doing differently?
- What might others be doing in response to my new behavior?
- How would I describe my new experience?

Reframing Exercises

6T

Re-frame your experience by stating in detail what you want instead of what you have, without complaining.

6u

Imagine this: You wake up tomorrow morning and everything related to this experience is exactly the way you'd like it to be.

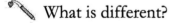 What is different?

6v

How would you view the day in the situation you just described?

6w

What would you be thinking, feeling, saying, and doing differently?

6x

What impact might a new viewpoint and a new approach have on key people around you?

Proclaiming

The fifth and final step in the Transformative Process™ is **Proclaiming** without restraining.

This is where commitment replaces intention—you translate desires into new action.

It's like writing the script of a movie with you starring in your new role, living the experience you desire from a fresh perspective with a new belief.

What are you saying to yourself, to others? How do you look and act differently? Write the kind of things you want to be proclaiming, as if they've already happened and you're describing them to a trusted friend.

Example

Proclaiming Without Restraining

In the team building session, members of the group compiled these proclamations:

"We came through the transition with flying colors. It was one of the best things that could have happened to us. We each developed powerful new leadership skills and learned what it means to create a supportive team by honoring our diverse approaches. We've begun celebrating one another's achievements and attained a whole new level of respect

within the company as we out-performed previous projections. It would be really hard to leave this team."

Remember, these proclamations were written before any of these things had transpired.

Intentions act as a compass, guiding energy toward chosen goals.

Affirmations 'firm up' visions of positive future events by claiming them as fact. They are written in the present tense, as if they have already happened.

Proclaiming Exercises

6Y

As if change has already happened, write a movie script in which you describe how transformation took place.

6z

What was a key moment or turning point for you in which you knew that personal transformation was underway?

6i

What change are you most proud of?

6ii

Write five statements of positive, personal proclamation to affirm your continued success. Write as if the transformation has already occurred.

Summary

Transformation is a lifelong process. It starts with a commitment to picking up the power tool of awareness with positive intentions, because we believe that we are responsible for, and worthy of creating a life worth living.

With awareness, we have the power to choose; the power to change; and the power to create empowering experiences—past, present, and future.

We transform our lives just five minutes at a time, by choosing positive points of view: naming, claiming, taming, reframing, and proclaiming new realities in thought, word, and deed.

Perhaps the rediscovery of our humanity, and the potential of the human spirit which we have read about in legends or older civilizations, or in accounts of solitary mystics, or in tales of science fiction writers~perhaps this will constitute the true revolution of the future. The new frontier lies not beyond the planets but within each one of us.
~Pierre Elliot Trudeau

Tool 7

Life-enriching Story Structure

Life-enriching Story Structure: Farewell to SOB Stories and SINS

Toolbox

**Full Circle Stories
tell about the gain from pain.
What happened?
So what? Now what?**

YOUR PAIN IS not your story. Your real story is the strength and skills you gained from your experiences.

Like the birth of a child, the labor is not really the story—people want to see the baby in all his or her glory.

> *If we give something our attention we rest
> our creativity on it...If we put our attention
> on the wrong things, they steal our energy
> and leave us impotent while pulling unsavory
> experiences into our lives.*
> *~Sonia Choquette*

It is said that the world is not made up of atoms, but of stories. An event or experience in itself is not a story. Full circle stories, like good art, portray motion and engender emotion. Something of significance changes.

The transformative story structure includes three distinct parts:

1. What happened?

2. So what?

3. Now what?

Life-enriching is a term that describes those things that add something positive to life.

When I've spent time and energy reading something, I want something back in exchange for what I have invested.

News stories often have a sensational slant. After reading or hearing a story in which I am exposed to grisly or inhuman events, I feel upset and slightly sick.

The ideals which have lighted my way, and time after time have given me new courage to face life cheerfully, have been kindness, beauty and truth.
                                                              ~Albert Einstein

When I pick up the power tool of awareness, I realize that I have the power to choose, the power to change, and the power to create life-enriching patterns of experience.

More and more, I use this question as a yardstick:

"Is this life-enriching for me?"

As a result, I may stop reading, switch channels, excuse myself from meaningless, negative conversations, or walk out of movies.

> *The kind of beauty I want most*
> *is the hard-to-get kind*
> *that comes from within-*
> *strength, courage, dignity.*
> *~Ruby Dee*

Example

What Happened?

At one time, writing was my way to vent pent-up pain, frustration, anger, alienation, loneliness, and hopelessness.

I filled notebooks and journals with what I call SOB Stories: Same Old Baloney.

They were about poor old me and my SINS: Self Inflicted Nonsense Stories.

I didn't know what else to do, so in its own way, this type of writing was helpful as an outlet.

Like a cat chasing its own tail, the same themes ran through stacks and stacks of my notebooks.

Although I invested vast amounts of time, energy, and money on many approaches to change, I still lived with the same SOB stories and SINS.

I could name the painful events of my inner, and, therefore, my outer world in detail. But after that I didn't know where to go. I was stuck.

The Transformative Process™ gave me a great gift. It took me by the pen and led me to the next steps of permanent change—the transformation I searched for but never found.

When I told my sister, Judy, that the Transformative Process™ was about life-enriching writing, her comment was, "For whom?"

This is an important question. Remember, the *Tools of Transformation* is not designed to help you write the next blockbuster or turn you into a literary genius. Your stories and writing through this process have a very different purpose.

The Transformative Process™ is a path to personal transformation and greater wholeness and balance. Your writing is for this purpose. Transformation is not about a product, but a life-long process. The writing that you produce is for you, even though you may share it with other people.

What anyone else thinks or feels or does with the discoveries you share with them is not the point. The important thing is what you've learned, and how you can use that to bring about new worlds of possibility for you.

Your personal discoveries and healing probably won't mean as much to other people as they do to you.

Even those nearest and dearest to you can be like the witnesses at the scene of the accident; because of who they are, they see things differently than you do, especially past events.

It's important to start by authentically and honestly naming our experiences; telling ourselves what happened, the event, beliefs, thoughts, and feelings.

The second step in the process of writing life-enriching stories requires adding the significance, or the meaning, we've given to what happened. This is what is meant by, "**So What?**"

Example

So What?

I was hired to work with the employees of a jewelry factory that was closing down. Each employee faced the same event. When they went home and told their families what happened the day they were notified of the plant closing, there were as many versions of what happened as there were employees.

John said, "What this means is that I'm finally free of this dead-end job. I haven't had the guts to leave in 18 years."

Charlie swore: "The bastards. I gave them 15 of the best years of my life and they toss me out like yesterday's garbage."

What Happened and So What are starting points, but pain, misfortune, or injury aren't the whole story.

Suffering and setbacks are a normal part of life. Misery, however, is optional.

After a major loss, it's natural to lose perspective. For a time, our whole world revolves around the loss.

Moving on is also natural. Each of us has his or her own timetable for recovery from loss. When people find it difficult to move on, it can help to find outside sources of support to put the event into a perspective we can live with.

In time, with determination, it is possible to recognize and focus on the gifts within even the most traumatic experience.

The point—the pulse of our story—is what we choose to do with what happens to us.

"Now What?" completes the story circle. Every storyteller hopes there will be something of value to him or her within the story. Otherwise, what's the point? How did what happened change you for the better?

Example

Now What?

When I met with a group of employees from the jewelry plant six months later, here's what I heard:

Joe went to a trade school and became a certified computer technician. When he told Charlie about the skills from the old job he was able to use in his new career, Charlie signed up for the same program.

"If we hadn't been let go, I'd still be bending over that workbench making rings. The company gave me and my family a better future by closing than they ever could by keeping me on."

Each person has the capacity to grow and recover even from the most traumatic experiences.

The process of change takes place on an individual timetable; some steps can take a very long time. Having a path to follow can make even devastating events more manageable.

Many people find that having these steps empowers them to take control of situations that have seemed beyond their control.

Summary: Full Circle Stories

When our stories progress from What Happened to So What, there's often a universal theme that human beings have dealt with throughout the ages.

When we reach Now What, the story has come full circle.

SOB—Same Old Baloney—stories and SINS—Self Inflicted Nonsense Stories—are noticeably absent.

Transformative stories are life-enriching. They show how problems that were faced gave birth to strengths, skills, insight, empathy, resolve, new directions, or decisions.

Story Structure Exercises

7A

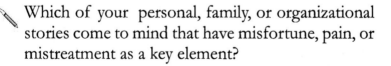 Which of your personal, family, or organizational stories come to mind that have misfortune, pain, or mistreatment as a key element?

Identify patterns that fall into the category of Same Old Baloney, featuring less than life-enriching experiences.

If you had to give these stories a descriptive label, what title would you give the general theme of these SOB stories?

If you were to do detective work, looking for possible Self Inflicted Nonsense Stories based on limiting or out-dated beliefs, what might you find?

7B

"What Happened?"

Name a single significant painful experience, without shame, and then claim it without blaming anyone, including yourself.

7c

Move on to "So What?"

Retelling SOB—Same Old Baloney—stories and SINS—Self Inflicted Nonsense Stories—depletes energy. When you're ready, move on to the next phase: the meaning you attached to the events, or their significance to you. This is So What?

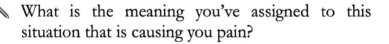 What is the meaning you've assigned to this situation that is causing you pain?

What are your underlying limiting beliefs that are making this so uncomfortable?

Example

Limiting Belief

Somewhere deep inside I knew I was an unwanted child, not just unplanned but unwanted—I was a real intrusion. At an early age I must have decided that my apology for just being here would be to be as independent and as helpful as I could.

Looking back, I can see the enormous role this single, outdated belief has had on my life, especially my relationships, but even my career. I've never been comfortable depending on anyone; I always thought I was too much of a burden, yet I love doing things for others.

It was very liberating to recognize that this belief caused lots of unnecessary adaptations. When I discovered it and replaced it with a new belief, long-term misery caused by my old belief began to fade away. When I let go of this self-inflicted nonsense, I had many more options than before.

When you're able to identify one limiting belief, you may recognize how many similar experiences are associated with it.

A good question to ask yourself is: **What would someone have to believe in order to have this experience?**

Friends of mine were separating, even though they loved each other. The night before they were to sign their divorce papers, Ted and I invited them to come to our house. We let them know that both of them would be there.

In one hour we explained how changing our beliefs had saved our marriage. As long as I believed that I couldn't count on Ted (or anyone), I kept seeing his behavior as evidence that I had to be independent to survive.

As long as Ted believed that it was impossible to please me, he experienced evidence that this was the case.

In fact, each of us had these beliefs long before the other came along, and we were like actors cast into a predictable role in the other's drama.

We explained to our friends that when we recognized the patterns caused by old, limiting beliefs, and changed them, everything changed. The closeness we had once felt returned. Remnants of our old beliefs still come up, especially when we're under stress, but we now recognize them for what they are. We're not controlled by them.

Our story struck a chord with our friends. They each identified the belief that they felt was at the core of their separation. They each wrote down these beliefs that they wanted to replace. Then they wrote their new beliefs on pieces of paper and put them on their fridge. They both worked at changing their old beliefs.

This couple went home together that night and are still together ten years later. I don't mean to suggest that changing beliefs is easy, but the dynamics of this process are fundamental steps that produce results.

7D

"Now What?"

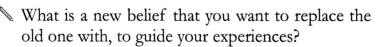 What is a new belief that you want to replace the old one with, to guide your experiences?

What might your life be like if you began to believe the positive belief you've identified?

7E

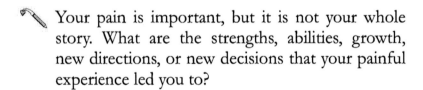

Your pain is important, but it is not your whole story. What are the strengths, abilities, growth, new directions, or new decisions that your painful experience led you to?

Example

Gains from Pain

One of the strengths I developed as a result of feeling unwanted and changing my belief about what that meant about me is realizing that other people need me as much as I need them. I now consciously do things for others out of love, not as a way of compensating them for allowing me to be here.

TOOL 8

Meet MIMI and Triggers

Meet MIMI and Triggers

Toolbox

Triggers are the keys that open four magical channels of creation:

Moments, Imagination, Memories, and Inspiration

ANY IMAGE, COMPARISON, picture, or object can become a Trigger—something that sets the flow of creativity in motion.

At Heartspace, we use a wide variety of objects as Triggers. At any class you might find the Trigger Table covered with photos or shoes; candy; mirrors; toys; paint color swatches; spices—you name it.

Triggers help access MIMI—shorthand initials for the four Transformative Channels:

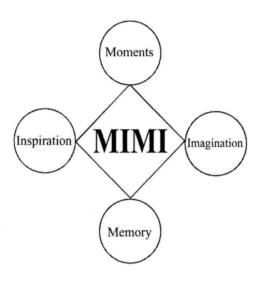

Picture creativity as a TV network named MIMI with a huge tuner with four basic channels: present Moments, Imagination, past Memories, and Inspiration.

Each channel has countless programs with sets, props, actors, and so on. People have their favorite channel that they habitually tune into.

Transformation requires tuning into a wider variety of channels to access different programs than the re-runs we're likely to see when we watch the same channel over and over.

Tuning into a different one of MIMI's transformative Channels can quickly lead to deeper insight and fresh intuitive connections—the heart of creativity.

Triggers are like Aladdin's lamp; they can lead you into unexplored worlds where anything can happen.

Here's a list of Triggers. You can use any one to enter deeper levels of awareness. You may choose to study the present moment as if it is under a magnifying glass, or step lightly into the world of fantasy and imagination, be moved by the magnet of memories, or rise to new heights on the wings of inspiration.

All of MIMI's Transformative Channels are yours to enjoy.

Invite your "Curious Creator"—the child you once were and still are—to come out and play.

Select one of these Triggers as your magic carpet for a five minute ride to new worlds of aliveness:

1. Photographs
2. Pictures, greeting cards, magazines, calendars
3. Plants
4. Animals
5. Clothing
6. Music
7. Food
9. Weather
10. Seasons
11. Holidays
12. Flowers
13. Special Events
14. Collections of things
15. Gifts
16. Travel
17. Colors
18. Smells
19. Sounds
20. School
21. Friends
23. Accidents
24. Buildings
25. Machines

Example

Triggering the Flow
Creative Connections

One Trigger can evoke many different responses. Cinnamon, for example, is a smell Rick remembers from the special buns his busy mom made that made him feel loved as a child.

The same word, Cinnamon, reminded me of a horse by the same name that I rode in the Grand Teton mountains 30 years ago. Another writer thought of a hair dye called Cinnamon that turned her hair a very odd color just before her son's wedding. Someone else thought Cinnamon would be a good name for a puppy they'd just brought home.

What memories, imaginary images, characters, thoughts, or stories does cinnamon trigger for you?

Writing short five-minute "story snapshots" from Triggers can be lots of fun, no matter which of MIMI's channels you use.

Example

Trigger - A Bone China Teacup

A Kitchen Memory

Mama and Aunt Jo are drinking Constant Comment tea from fancy, breakable, decorated china teacups with saucers at our kitchen table. Our family uses turquoise melmac dishes; only Mom and Aunt Jo use the cups from high on the shelf. They get to have spice cake with raisins and white frosting, called Spanish Slice, that Mama got at the Kroger store, just for her and Aunt Jo.

They're laughing at one of Aunt Jo's funny stories about St. Joe hospital, where Mom and Jo are both nurses. Aunt Jo is big. Her calves remind me of turkey drumsticks. Her hair is so thin her pink scalp peeks through. She's kind of gruff, but Mom melts her like a sugar cube, just like she does everyone else, with hugs and love. Aunt Jo is Mama's best friend, and she's beautiful to her.

My heart smiled when I saw Aunt Jo come through the door today because I knew Mom will be happy and stop working. She'll be busy with Aunt Jo so she won't be asking me to do things to help out.

Maybe today Mom will let me have a cup of tea and a bit of slice. I never get to stay long because they want to talk about secret grown-up things like husbands and gossip.

Hurray! They invited me to sit with them. While it lasts it's like finding a pot of gold at the end of the rainbow.

© Joanne Klassen 11:03 a.m. 10/21/02 Winnipeg

Triggers are the remote control buttons to MIMI's Transformative Channels.

As we visit the present moment with greater awareness, we can discover things we've overlooked.

> **You never know when you're making a memory.**
> **~Rickie Lee Jones**

Memories are stored in sensory detail. When we use a Trigger to take us to a memory, many accompanying details are sure to follow, like the tail on a kite.

A single Trigger can breathe new worlds of Imagination into being, instantly.

When we focus deeply on a single Trigger, Inspiration, like a butterfly to a flower, is sure to join us.

179

MIMI & Story Snapshots

*If one is lucky, a solitary fantasy can totally trans-
form one million realities.*
~*Maya Angelou*

8A

Select a Trigger and write a Freestyle "story snapshot" of what the Trigger led you to.

8B

When you finish your five-minute story snapshot, before moving on, pause to reflect on the Transformative Channels you tuned into.

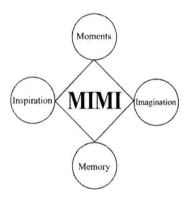

Is the channel you wrote from one you tend to tune into often?

If so, what might you gain from exploring other channels?

If not, what did you like about writing from this channel?

When I was younger, I could remember anything,
whether it happened or not.
~Mark Twain

8c

Select a new Trigger and answer these questions:

What drew me to this Trigger (image, comparison, picture, or object)?

What about this is important to me? Which of my values does it remind me of?

How did I come to value this?

How have I expressed this value in my life, relationships, or career?

Why is this value significant to me now?

8D

Write a reminder about any discoveries you made in connection to the today's Trigger and your life.

Example

Triggers and Comparisons

Kermit the frog, on this greeting card, reminds me that my uniqueness is OK. I can enjoy being me without fear. No one sees the world exactly as I do, so my view is what I possess, my gift. If I try to be like everyone else in order to measure up to some imagined standard to fit in, my energy, my aliveness sink like a stone. If I want to vibrate with joy, I must be me.

TOOL 9

Gems & a String of Story Pearls

Gems & a String of Story Pearls

*Use what talents you possess; the woods would be
very silent if no birds sang except
those that sang best.*
~Henry Van Dyke

Purpose

PEARLS HAVE ALWAYS been valued as objects of
beauty. It takes an oyster years to turn the irritant
of a single grain of sand into a pearl. Divers travel
to the depths of the ocean to retrieve the most
priceless pearls. In this Tool you'll create your own
priceless string of Pearls, story by story, as you link
shining memories with moments of inspiration.

The goal of Story Pearls is to zero in on prime
events and relationships that have shaped your
life. Pearls often contain universal themes like risk,
love, learning, loss, and letting go. Pearls provide
a specific focus or intentional target that helps
writing flow.

Pearls give valuable new insight into life-shaping
experiences. Pearls help you make friends with
forgotten pieces of yourself that may guide your
decision making.

I recently realized that companies, families, organizations, groups, and communities have strings of Story Pearls that can serve similar functions to the Story Pearls that make up an individual life.

One day you must tell me your full and complete story...It's extremely important because it helps to remind yourself of who you are. Then you can go forward, without fear of losing yourself in this ever-changing world.
~Rohinton Mistry

Pearls often begin as a few paragraphs and become stories, poetry, songs, or fiction. At the start, it's important to allow the Pearl to take the shape it wants to. Later, you can polish it with special emphasis on feelings and details, like a jeweler brings luster to a stone.

How to Write Pearls

Read down the list of Pearls. One of the titles is likely to appeal to you more than others. The order in which you complete Pearls is not important. Select a Pearl that speaks to you or where you feel energized; I call it "heat." Which stories want to push their way into the front of your mind? You may start writing about one thing, only to find yourself writing about something entirely different.

Start by describing a specific single image.

To help you get started, you can just write, or you may want to review what you've written in your notebook, your previous J5M and J10M exercises, to see if there is a seed Pearl you'd like to expand and deepen.

Here's a list of the types of story "Pearls" you may want to write about:

1. GEMS: Greatest Experienced Moments to Savor

2. Peaks: Mountain Top Moments of Clarity

3. Turning Points: Things were never the same...

4. Valleys: Low Points—the Hardest Parts

5. Stepping Stones: From Certainty to Uncertainty

6. Simple Pleasures: Moments of Magic

7. Lighthouses: Bright Lights in Dark Moments

8. Unsung Heroes: They made a BIG difference

A Step Further

Pearls lend themselves to special treatment. Like getting dressed up for a special occasion, there's fun in feeling you are presenting your best self to your best advantage. Here are some ways writers have "decked out" their Pearls when they finished writing:

- Dorothy added mementos to her Pearls: a lace handkerchief, pressed flowers.

- Edith uses photographs to focus her Pearls as she writes, and as finishing touches when she's done.

- Peggy and Doris add their sketches, doodles, or artwork to their Pearls.

- I like to use fancy paper and add borders, computer graphics and stickers to my Pearls. I slide them into plastic page protectors for safekeeping.

Recipes, maps, color—literally whatever you can dream up that reflects you, can be added to make your Pearls come alive.

Your string of Story Pearls will give you the start of a personal portfolio of writing that can be helpful in career planning or relationship building. For now, the important thing is to just write. Later, you can decide who, where, when, and how you may want to share your writing. The goal of a Pearl is to delight the writer within and remind you of the best of who you are, a priceless, irreplaceable being, with unique experiences of infinite variety and value.

GEMS

GEMS, shorthand for Greatest Experienced Moments to Savor, are memory moments that bring a smile to your face. GEMS result in flashes of aliveness. Recalling GEMS moves a positive warm glow instantly through your body, bathing your cells in the chemical response to pleasure. The body does not distinguish between vividly imagined events from long ago and events taking place right now.

GEMS are a great addition to your awareness notebook or journal. Add GEMS as you remember them or as they occur. This is one of the most energizing types of writing, a good Pearl to begin with.

Sometimes one GEM will lead to another and a larger story is born. For example, a GEM for me was hearing the driver of our bus announce to Ted's hockey team and their spouses on a trip through Austria, "Ladies and Gentlemen, you are now entering the Alps." Wow, I never thought I'd be in the Alps. Later in the week, I had my first ski lesson on a glacier high on a mountain peak. Another Greatest Experienced Moment to Savor.

GEMS are tiny memory moments, sparks of imagination, or inspiration jewels waiting to be written about and enjoyed. GEMS are not full-blown stories in themselves, they're more like snapshots of special moments, or pictures that would fit on a postcard. They naturally lead to wanting to write more at another time.

GEMS are the ultimate in "feel good" personal writing.

GEMS Exercises

9A

Begin by writing a list of some of the most beautiful places and things you've ever seen, heard, or felt.

What are some of your favorite things people have said to or about you?

What are some of the best surprises or gifts life has bestowed upon you?

What do you love to do?

Who do you most like to be with?

Which of your accomplishments are you most proud of?

Many GEMS have helped bring you to where you are today. Which ones come to mind at this time?

Select a single Trigger to begin: an object, symbol, sense, word, or emotion. Write Freestyle about GEMS for J5M / J10M.

Closing: What did you receive from writing about GEMS?

Peak, or Mountain Top Experiences

At the top of a mountain, the air is exhilarating. You can see in all directions. There is a sense of accomplishment and a clarity of vision that exists nowhere else.

In peak experiences we come face to face with a power much greater than ourselves.
~Hal Zina Bennett

Peak Experience Excercises

9B

Many Peak Experiences have helped bring you to where you are today. Which ones come to mind at this time?

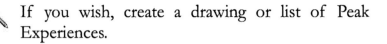 If you wish, create a drawing or list of Peak Experiences.

Select a single Trigger to begin: an object, symbol, sense, word, or emotion. Write Freestyle for J5M / J10M.

Closing: What did you receive from writing about this Peak Experience?

As you write about a Peak Experience, you may wish to go deeper and experiment with including more Transformative Tools. A checklist of questions is provided at the end of this Tool.

Turning Points

Things were never the same.

> *Memories are the key not to the past,*
> *but to the future.*
> ~*Corrie Ten Boom*

There are so many turning points in the course of a life. Some are chosen, others are thrust on us. If you think of your life's journey as a road map (you may want to draw it as one), you'll discover many turning points along the way: Births, deaths, moves, losses, firsts, decisions, and places where the road behind was as good as washed out—there was no turning back.

Turning Points Exercises

9c

Of the many turning points that have shaped the course of your life, which ones come to mind at this time?

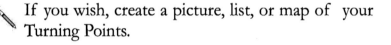 If you wish, create a picture, list, or map of your Turning Points.

197

Select a single Trigger to begin: an object, symbol, sense, word, or emotion. Write Freestyle for J5M / J10M.

Closing: What did you receive from writing about this Turning Point?

As you write about a Turning Point in your life, you may wish to go deeper and experiment with including more Transformative Tools. A checklist of questions is provided at the end of this Tool.

Valleys

In the depth of winter I finally learned that
there was in me an invincible summer.
~Albert Camus

Valleys are life's lowest points where clouds of fear, aloneness, despair, pain, or sadness block the sunshine from our field of vision. In retrospect, valleys can show us how our greatest set backs, mistakes, defeats, injuries, and what Hal Zina Bennett calls "Essential wounds," led to victories and strengths that could have come to us no other way.

...perhaps all the dragons of our lives are
princesses waiting to see us as beautiful and brave.
~Rainer Maria Rilke

Valley Exercises

9D

Many Valley experiences have helped shape the person you are today. Which ones come to mind at this time?

If you wish, create a picture or list of Valleys.

Select a single Trigger to begin: an object, symbol, sense, word, or emotion. Write Freestyle for J5M / J10M.

Closing: What did you receive from writing about this Valley?

As you write about a Valley, you may wish to go deeper and experiment with including more Transformative Tools. A checklist of questions is provided at the end of this Tool.

Stepping Stones

Risks lead us from certainty to uncertainty.

> *Why not go out on a limb?*
> *Isn't that where the fruit is?*
> *~Frank Scully*

Some Stepping Stones are like the slippery rocks we stepped out on to cross the river, hoping they'd hold us so we could reach the other shore safely.

Other Stepping Stones carry us to more distant shores. I remember thinking, when I moved from Ann Arbor, Michigan to Winnipeg, Manitoba, in 1975, "Will I sink or stay afloat in this vast northern sea of unknowns?" My lifeboat was, as yet, untested. My Stepping Stone Story Pearls make up a large section of my portfolio.

What are the risks you've taken? I'm told we fell down several hundred times before we successfully took our first baby step unaided. The nature of risk is not knowing how a decision will turn out. Mortgages, jobs, relationships, education, starting a business, taking a trip—they all involve risks.

Stepping Stones Exercises

9E

Many Stepping Stones have helped shape the course of your life. Which ones come to mind at this time?

If you wish, create a picture, list, or flow chart of Stepping Stones.

Select a single Trigger to begin: an object, symbol, sense, word, or emotion. Write Freestyle for J5M / J10M.

Closing: What did you receive from writing about this Stepping Stone?

As you write about a Stepping Stone, you may wish to go deeper and experiment with including more Transformative Tools. A checklist of questions is provided at the end of this Tool.

Simple Pleasures

There are moments of magic that come from the simplest of things, like rainbows and laughter, to brighten the ordinary.

> *Seize from every moment its unique novelty, and do not prepare your joy.*
> *~Andre Guide*

It's often not the elaborate or expensive versions of fun or entertainment that provide the greatest pleasure. Like a child enjoying soap bubbles or a fort made from a cardboard box, moments of magic from the past live on in simple pleasures.

My husband loves reading the comics in the Sunday paper. I relish a cup of hot chocolate with a marshmallow. What past associations do you have with simple pleasures that make them special?

With a little detective work, you'll find Story Pearls behind Simple Pleasures, waiting to be told.

Simple Pleasures Exercises

9F

Many Simple Pleasures have shaped the person you are today, forming the things that can turn an ordinary moment into a magical one. Which Simple Pleasures come to mind at this time?

If you wish, create a list or picture of Simple Pleasures.

Select a single Trigger to begin: an object, symbol, sense, word, or emotion. Write Freestyle for J5M / J10M.

Closing: What did you receive from writing about Simple Pleasures?

As you write about Simple Pleasures, you may wish to go deeper and experiment with including more Transformative Tools. A checklist of questions is provided at the end of this Tool.

Lighthouses

Bright Lights in Dark Moments

> *Never hesitate to hold out your hand;*
> *never hesitate to accept*
> *the outstretched hand*
> *of another.*
> *~Pope John XXIII*

While traveling in New Orleans, I got on a city bus in rush hour and the door closed, separating me from my daughter. When I tried to get off it was too late.

A woman beside me on that crowded bus noticed my distress and went out of her way to get off at the next stop and get me headed in the right direction to find my daughter. I'll never forget her face.

When I reflect on that experience, I'm suddenly back on that bus with tears spilling down my cheeks. The lighthouse of a stranger's kindness was like a beacon in a fierce storm. Like an angel, she spoke to me—her voice and her hand on my shoulder were a light I will always remember.

Lighthouses Exercises

9G

Many bright lights have appeared in dark moments to shape the person you are today. What are some Lighthouse experiences that come to mind at this time?

If you wish, create a list or picture of Lighthouse experiences.

Select a single Trigger to begin: an object, symbol, sense, word, or emotion. Write Freestyle for J5M / J10M.

Closing: What did you receive from writing about this Lighthouse?

As you write about a Lighthouse, you may wish to go deeper and experiment with including more Transformative Tools. A checklist of questions is provided at the end of this Tool.

Unsung Heroes:
People who Made a BIG Difference

Without heroes, we are all plain people
and don't know how far we can go.
~Bernard Malamud

Can you remember back to your childhood heroes? Maybe they were cowboys, as many of mine were, or perhaps athletes, storybook characters, or movie stars.

Unsung Heroes Exercises

9H

Many Unsung Heroes that never reached the public eye have helped bring you to where you are today. Who comes to mind at this time?

If you wish, create a picture or list of Unsung Heroes. Photographs can help with this Story Pearl.

Select a single Trigger to begin: an object, symbol, sense, word, or emotion. Write Freestyle for J5M / J10M.

Closing: What did you receive from writing about your Unsung Hero?

As you write about your Unsung Hero, you may wish to go deeper and experiment with including more Transformative Tools. A checklist of questions is provided at the end of this Tool.

Here's a Story Pearl I wrote about my paternal grandmother. I put it in my personal portfolio along with other Story Pearls. I'd like to share this one with you. It's about someone I'd like you to meet.

Example

Story Pearl

An Unsung Heroine - Alzina Hindal
Of Garber, Strawberry Point, and Des Moines, Iowa

If you met Alzina Feidt Hindal, my grandmother, you'd notice that everything about her from the outside was quite ordinary. If you could see beneath her surface you'd discover that Alzina loved beauty and utility.

She spent countless hours finding lovely patterns and skimping to buy supplies for endless crocheting and quilting projects, created in between family and household responsibilities. If we put all her beautiful handiwork together it would fill rooms—in fact, it does today, in the homes of her 10 children, grandchildren, great, and great-great grandchildren.

One of my fondest memories of Grandma's love of utility happened one 94-degree Iowa day—a day where the humidity exceeded the heat. A good corn-growing day. Grandma had lost Grandpa a few years before when he died during a gall bladder operation. She slowed down, almost to a crawl, until a pacemaker helped boost her heart, and her zest for life returned like a robin in spring.

I picture Grandma sitting on a threadbare sofa on her porch as her son Art, an accountant, arrives with some startling news. Grandma's only brother, a poor bachelor farmer, passed away earlier that year. Art's news is about an inheritance Grandma received from the sale of her brother's land.

"Mom, guess what?" Art tells her that she's received a hefty inheritance. Almost more money than she can imagine. His eyes scan the shabby porch. "What's the first thing you'd like to do with the money?"

Grandma says something about dividing it up for her kids. They'd all chipped in for years to help out. Art asks, "But what about you?"

Her face slowly lights up in a half-smile as she gestures with her hand. "I'd like one of those electric fans that goes..." She moves her hand back and forth like an oscillating fan.

Here's a woman who can have anything she wants, and she picks a $25 fan to create a nice breeze on a sweltering day. That's my grandma.

I also remember Christmas week in Michigan, where I grew up. We three kids would run to the window whenever a delivery van pulled up; it could be Grandma Hindal's box. The biggest treat inside lay hidden in an empty Christmas card box carefully lined with red tissue paper: Grandma's creamy white candy with black walnuts.

Mom rationed that candy like gold dust. Fifty years later, my mouth still waters thinking about the fruit of grandmother's labor and love—a beautiful taste to enjoy for a moment, but remember forever.

Other gifts in Grandma's box were expressions of her love of utility, like two pairs of Buster Brown cotton anklets for me. Navy and green—a good choice for not showing the dirt, but disappointing to a teenager. The girls at school were wearing only white crew socks that year.

Looking back, I see how easy it was to undervalue the special qualities of my grandma. She wasn't always up on the latest trends, but her timeless love for each of us shines brightly across the generations.

Reflecting on Alzina's gifts, from the perspective of grandmotherhood, I discover that her love of family, beauty and utility is a living legacy that's become an essential part of me, and so many of her offspring.

For the everlasting, treasured inheritance she left me, I offer this tribute to Alzina Hindal, my grandma, a much cherished, unsung heroine.

© Joanne Klassen, July 20, 2002
Belair, MB 12 noon, 94 degrees

Diving Deeper...

Here's a checklist that includes many tools of transformation. Ask yourself these questions as you complete your string of Story Pearls.

☐ Did I include aspects of the Anatomy of an Experience?

   Events, Perceptions, Beliefs, Thoughts, Emotions, Sensations, Actions, and Reactions.

☐ What about Story Structure?
   —What happened? So What? Now What?

☐ Did challenges give birth to new strengths, skills, beliefs, attitudes, actions, or direction?

☐ Have I used the Transformative Process™?

   Named it without shame?
   Claimed it without blame?
   Tamed it without complaining?
   Reframed it without explaining?
   Proclaimed it without restraining?

☐ Are there special touches I could add?

☐ Who, if anyone, would I really like to share this with? What would be the best way for me to do that?

A Final thought on Story Pearls

I believe our stories are precious, irreplaceable, treasure.

My friend Norm told me one evening at an annual meeting that, like me, he planned to write his stories, when he retired in a few years.

Norm had a fascinating life with more careers and interests than I could count. At the time he was employed as an addictions counsellor.

Norm said, "I think telling my stories may help someone somewhere, someday. I know that telling my stories will help me move into the next chapter of my life, whatever that is."

Norm died suddenly the next day, taking all of his stories with him. The day after his funeral I woke up with the vision that led me to start Heartspace Writing School. When I write a story that reminds me of Norm, I wish he were here to share some of his with me.

TOOL 10

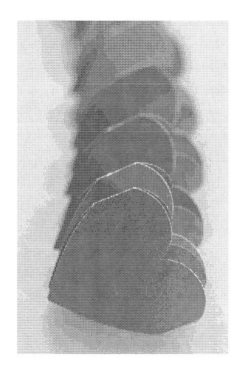

Combining Tools
~An Illustration

Combining Tools–
An Illustration

Linking Transformative Tools

Toolbox

Pick the tools you think will help you will do the job, but whatever you do, get started.

AT THE START of the book, I mentioned that the tools of transformation are as versatile as duct tape. Used alone, you can make magic with them; combine them, and you never know what you'll create.

> *I think what we're seeking is an*
> *experience of being alive.*
> *~Joseph Campbell*

I was recently asked for a longer version of an example of how I've used the tools to transform my world. Here's an example of what started as a J5M morning writing. I ended up writing for the better part of an hour. In that time I transformed several aspects of a corner of my world, as you can see.

*It's only a thought,
and a thought can be changed.
~Louise L. Hay
(one of my personal heroes)*

Step One

Trigger - Weather

Moments Channel

If I were weather today I'd be 72-degree sunshine and a whisper of a breeze, kissing children's foreheads.

Step Two

Shift to Memory Channel

The kind of day when I was a kid and I gobbled life up, grabbing handfuls from first eyes open to last surrender to sweet dreams.

Step Three

Imagination Channel

I'd like to live where this kind of weather is the rule, not the exception. Maybe In La Jolla, where Ted could play golf 300 days a year and thrive.

Step Four
Inspiration Channel

The idea of a constant temperature and perfect weather reminds me of the not-so-sunny number we heard this week. I long for no clouds and sunshine, with perfect numbers like 72-degree weather. Ted's PSA, a marker for prostate cancer, climbed to 66 this week. It's up 10 points, an indication that cancer may be spreading despite all his efforts.

Step Five
Intention and Affirmation

What is my intention? I want to feel sunny, carefree as a child, and upbeat to cheer my husband despite my cold and feeling like an ice flow separates us. I'd like to wake up and find the sky clear, life waiting to be gobbled up, instead of the spare vegan diet we have been attempting.

I'd like a fresh, reassuring breeze to kiss my forehead, a sign that the weather ahead is promising.

I claim and affirm an attitude of gratitude for strength, blessings, health and wholeness, right here and right now. And so it is.

Write On - J5M - Story Snapshot
What is asking me to acknowledge it?

A Recent Dream

Last night I dreamed about a little girl—Terina's new baby whose name I didn't know, so I said "her." I found out she was called Jenna. No one seemed to pay attention to her till I heard noise like tissue paper crumpling, then this wee baby was out of her bed and had made a mess upstairs.

No one was too concerned with her. In fact, she wasn't hurting or ruining anything; it was a harmless mess that needed to be cleaned up. Her mom, Terina, was tired, so I said I'd tidy everything up. I told Jenna she wasn't bad, she was just being what she was, a baby.

She had our attention now. My brother Don, Terina's dad, and his wife Lynda were staying in the spare room. The baby took something valuable that I put back in their bedroom.

I wonder if the baby was cancer? I didn't know its name. It got our attention. I am trying to clean up the mess. It's not bad, it is what it is.

The cancer, as a matter of course, took something valuable from our bedroom—lovemaking—I put it back. Terina represents someone else, not directly our nuclear family but someone close to me. Bad things have happened to her this year—Randy's unhealed ankle injury—and also to Don and Lynda—Matt's suicide. Now it's our home. It always seemed like cancer happened to other people—it would not touch us.

Transformative Process™

Name it - without shame

What is my honest experience today? I am blown over by cancer growing in Ted's body and evidence that our best efforts have not been enough to reverse its course. I am trying to clean up something that is beyond my control and ability. I am chilled to the bone when I feel this powerless.

Claim it - without blame

This is not about anyone or anything except me, my fear of not being in control. It's a life-long issue. Because of it, I hate to admit I need anyone, that they are essential to my well being. I love Ted completely. He is the center of my world. I need him in so many ways. I have tried to plan my life and act so as to control the forces that impact me—to do all I can to ensure sunny days for me and mine.

Tame it - without complaining

I know I need to name my fears. What would I have to believe to be having this experience of recent events? I stumble on a deep-down fear: that I don't deserve all the wonderful things I have in my life.

I haven't worked hard enough, been good enough. I harbor unconscious fear that maybe, like Job in the Bible, everything I value can be taken away no matter what I do.

Reframe it - without explaining

What do I want to believe, and therefore, experience, instead of this? I want to plant my feet, my mind, my heart and spirit on the sunlit path of faith. I want to abandon the dark, cold, alone place of fear.

I hear the words of my Sunday school days, "It is your Father's good pleasure to give you the kingdom in its fullness." And Jesus saying, "Of my self I can do nothing." And, "With God all things are possible to them that believe."

I know that when I touch the truth it truly sets my fear free and my day is sunny. I choose to believe that I am worthy of love. I pray for healing of the limited perceptions in which fear dwells.

Proclaim it - without restraining

How can my thinking, feeling, and behavior reflect what I want so I can leave behind what I don't want? I affirm that my world is a celebration of aliveness, without judgment, which makes every day perfect weather, no matter what the temperature or forecast says. There are gifts in every situation.

I claim the gifts of this time, different than I expected, but rich gifts all the same, full of opportunity for new closeness, learning, compassion, understanding, and strengthened faith. All is well in my world. I am not alone. I can face this and ask for help or listening and support. Fear is not invited here.

De-briefing with Story Structure

What happened?

I responded to a Trigger about weather. I'd be a sunny, perfect, no clouds day, and realized I idealize sunshine. Ted and I in sunshine, retired, golfing, writing in La Jolla. Storm clouds blew over—his elevated PSA test results, cancer possibly spreading. This touched off fear; I faced it, and got my feet back on the solid path of my faith.

So What?

I feel lighter, freer. I feel like I am not traveling alone. Instead of fear nipping at my heels, just outside of my awareness, dragging me down, I am on top of the wholeness of my inner experience and can steer clear of fear's pull.

Now What?

My cold is clearing for the first time in over a week. As I choose to see the perfection in what is, I am at peace. Energy returns like a gentle breeze kissing my forehead. Life is a mirror, reflecting information to me, not doom. Cancer, as they say, is a word. It need not be a sentence. My resolve to center myself in faith is strengthened. I'm smiling.

Writing this book has been a peak experience for me. It has given me bushels of joy to introduce you to the *Tools of Transformation.*

I hope that the Anatomy of an Experience, the Transformative Process™, and these exercises and examples provide you with a durable toolbox of choices to use, five minutes at a time, to transform your world.

 It is my belief that each of us is absolutely worthy of, and responsible for, helping create our world with the precious gift of free will. For me, using the Transformative Process™ is like holding hands with God.

I wish you many blessings and bountiful awareness on your life's journey.

It is within my power either to serve God or not to serve him. Serving him, I add to my own good and the good of the whole world. Not serving him, I forfeit my own good and deprive the world of that good, which was in my power to create.
~Leo Tolstoy

A Bouquet of Thanks

MANY MIDWIVES HELPED this book as it traveled from a twinkle in my eye into the world. Each pair of helping hands, each careful thought and edit, and each encouraging word made publication possible.

Special thanks to Nina Lee Colwill, world-class friend and editor. For family support, editing, meals, and massage delivered to my desk, I thank Ty Klassen, Anna Rojas Flores, Tiffany Elliott, and Ted Klassen. Book Me In buddies, and Rick Johnson, a big thank you.

The creative contributions of Lynne Forbes, Darlene and Michael Schacht of Art Book Bindery, Jan Funk, and "Dr." Dawn Wilson of Interior Publishing & Communication, and Terry Harapiak, helped bring this book through the final birthing stages right on our due date. To each of you, many bouquets of thanks.

About Joanne Klassen

JOANNE KLASSEN, B.Sc., President of Heartspace International Associates, has pioneered holistic programs for organizational, personal, and business development.

Joanne has taught on the continuing education faculties of the University of Manitoba, University of Winnipeg, Red River and Assiniboine Community Colleges; the Niagara Institute; and Management Concepts of Washington, D.C.

She has designed and delivered 3,000 board and staff training sessions, and career transition programs for organizations such as: The City of Winnipeg, United Grain Growers, Investors Group, Jostens, Manitoba Blue Cross, Atomic Energy Commission, United Steelworkers, Inter-Tribal Child and Family Services, many school divisions, and the Business Development Bank of Canada.

Joanne is the author of books, workbooks, articles, poetry, and *The Family Tree* board game. Her first book, *Learning to Live, Learning to Love*, has been translated and distributed worldwide.

In 1998, she founded Heartspace Writing School to introduce Transformative Writing and the Transformative Process™—roadmaps to self-discovery through personal story telling.

She lives in Winnipeg, Manitoba, Canada with her husband Ted. Their five children, grandchildren, golf, church, and midnight writing keep her feet on the ground when her head is in the clouds.

Joanne Klassen offers 30 different workshops for individuals, groups, and organizations, including Facilitator training in the Transformative Process™.

Contact Joanne at:
jklassen@write-away.net or
www.write-away.net

Student Reflections

"I am in awe of this process. The tools fan an inner flame."
—Roseanne Keyes, Heartspace graduate, author of *A Place on the Totem Pole.*

"Imagine writing in a group where you feel completely safe. Imagine writing easily and effortlessly with others who receive and honor the gift of your words—your essence. Imagine enjoying the sheer beauty of words. This became a reality for me at Heartspace."
—Madeleine Enns, Teacher

"No matter how personal, our writing is universal and resonates profoundly. Heartspace is an incredible gift I gave myself."
—Pierre Guérin, CBC Radio producer.

"I've grown more peaceful with who I am and who I'm becoming."
—Laura McClelland, former banker, mother of 3.

Order additional copies
of Tools of Transformation at:

INFI(∞)ITY
PUBLISHING.COM
www.buybooksontheweb.com
Toll-free (877) BUY-BOOK
Local Phone (610) 941-9999
Fax (610) 941-9959

Order *Learning to Live, Learning to Love*,
by Joanne Klassen
at: Jalmar Press,
1-800-662-9662
www.jalmarpress.com

Lightning Source UK Ltd.
Milton Keynes UK
14 February 2010
150069UK00001B/36/A